Quartet for Three Voices

Quartet for Three Voices

p o e m s

James Applewhite

Louisiana State University Press
Baton Rouge 2002

Designer: Amanda McDonald Scallan
Typeface: Bembo
Typesetter: Coghill Composition, Inc.
Printer and binder: Thomson-Shore, Inc.

Library of Congress Cataloging-in-Publication Data:
Applewhite, James.
    Quartet for three voices : poems / James Applewhite.
      p. cm.
    ISBN 0-8071-2773-6 (Hardcover : alk. paper)—ISBN 0-8071-2774-4 (Paperback : alk. paper)
    I. Title.
    PS3551.P67 Q37 2002
    811'.54—dc21

    2001005167

The paper in this book meets the guidelines for permanence and durability of the Committee on Production Guidelines for Book Longevity of the Council on Library Resources. ∞

Poems appeared in the following publications: "Bells for Cecilia" and "Space at the Table," *Sewanee Review* vol. 107, no. 4 (Fall 1999); "The Book of Evening," *Sewanee Review* vol. 108, no. 2 (Spring 2000); "Charles," *Hudson Review* vol. 52, no. 3 (Autumn 1999); "Conversation in Faculty Commons," *Faculty Forum* (Duke University) vol. 13, no. 2 (November 2, 2001); "Documentary," *Oxford American* no. 41 (Fall 2001); "The Headlines Fade," *American Studies in Scandinavia* vol. 33, no. 2 (2001); "Quartet for Three Voices," under the title "Circle of Light," *Vanderbilt Review* 16 (2000); "Snapshot of Jonquils," *Oxford American* (January–February 1999); "Southern Humor," *Brightleaf: A Southern Review of Books* vol. 1 (September–October 1997); "The Southerner in Space after Death" and "White Lake Last Light," *Hampden-Sydney Poetry Review,* 25th Anniversary Issue (Winter 2000); "Timothy McVeigh at Heaven's Gate," *Poetry Review* vol. 88, no. 1 (Spring 1998). "The Wizard of Oz," Southern Review vol. 35, no. 3 (Summer 1999); "The Word Father," *Solo: A Journal of Poetry* no. 4 (December–January 2001/2); "Yates Mill Wheel," *Raleigh (N.C.) News and Observer,* July 2, 2000.

Contents

Quartet for Three Voices

The Word Father

> "The question is," said Alice, "whether you *can* make
> words mean so many different things."

Your word of loss glosses all air, spot
      like a blindness when I've stared into sun.
I call you Humpty Dumpty, old card, heart-
           king in ermine and maroon.

O mirror shaped like a man, your *beyond*
      is silver thin, leaving me no plan to stand—
though live flowers discuss my fate, in voices
           that pass like breaths on glass.

Asking me what's in a name, you resign
      your kingdom for this surface of sign
that reverses my land: far atmosphere
           naming me your infinite heir.

I run with the Red Queen, endure
      the logic of a chessboard nature—
standing still though the squares are hurled
           into dark by a turning world.

Old ghost, your footsteps letter the distance
      toward a coast inscribed *No Entrance.*
I follow your alphabet, read the cross-
           coordinates that locate loss.

Christ weeps on his tree musically—
      unfathered like me, human on one side only—
eye on fire for all beyond, divinity inventing
           a script in air for the missing.

Quartet for Three Voices

A phone call played on our heartstrings,
        word from his lights among shanties
that we would be three a little longer.
                Darkies were our friends they said,

who wore red headcloths as if to bind old wounds
        and blue and violet clothes over violent laughter.
Their throatings came mellow from afar. Inside, the houses
                smelled of a kerosene flicker, yellow,

of collards and fatback frying. Their sayings
        stitched our screen wire with brighter notes,
wove in their laughter—those whose meager livings
                shaped our fates and our wealths,

their wrinkles grinning or strain-lines lifting
        scribed by ripples in the river-face, like grain
of packhouse siding—their tones of skin as if rained-
                on galvanized roofs of barns

russet with decades. Our eyes knew each other
        in our floating circle, supported by their current
below us. Such differences as walled us from them
                seemed to us children flimsy

and wooden, our houses adrift like theirs on war
        and storm. Fear spread our smiles so wide
across the sides of this ritual divide, between our
                fingers that rotated the drumstick,

theirs that wrung the chicken's neck or heaved the ax.
        Who were our people we wondered, as our father
like a sentry guarded his gas pumps.
                His strict pediment of lights

defended our identity against a shanty
        town surrounding in concentric rings, rich
with the gold-foiled condoms he'd sold while
                moths beat wings at his wattage.

His lit columns left us in darkness,
        all of us brothers, incomplete. Staring through
the just-closed door, we heard its one spring
                humming an elegy of absence.

Timothy McVeigh at Heaven's Gate

Celibate as Timothy McVeigh in his cell,
        these celebrities led by Marshall Applewhite
await their spacecraft. The millennium comes,
                Heaven's Gate the Hale-Bopp comet.

Paranoias accelerate. Surreal explosions bring on
        the Big One. The chip's in your buttock, they see
you on space TV, crack shots tracking your ass. Skin-
            heads zigzag their U.S. in black paint.

The war game boys have tunneled deep into where
        we think. Who imagined the helicopters black?
Who'll guide the UN in? Our strength cometh from
            uranium, from silos under peaks.

Fascist militias march this consciousness where my
        mild, mad namesake dispensed his barbiturate
poetry. Surfeited on PCs, they haloed heads with plastic
           bags, inhaling a cometary coma.

Fertile America teems with bombs, farm
        of arrogant masteries, gargantuan as myth.
Some are willing to lie down and die with us.
           Their faith is guns. Don't laugh

at the embrace. Those patriots my quiet ones fled
        trained to kill at a distance. He watched a life
he'd nailed across hairs of a gunsight, then squeezed—
           bursting his heart, and his country's.

Interstate Highway
for our daughter, Lisa

As on a crowded Interstate the drivers in boredom
        or irritation speed ahead or lag (taken with sudden
enthusiasms for seventy-five), surging ahead a little by
            weaving between lanes but still

staying pretty much even, so too the seeker in language
        ranges ahead and behind—exiting and rejoining
a rushing multitude so closely linked that,
            if seen from above, from the height

of the jet now descending, we present one
        stasis of lights: feeling our freedom though
when seen from above, in the deepening twilight,
            the pattern we bead is constant.

So we have traveled in time, lying down and waking
        together, moved by illusions, each cubicle with
tables and chairs, beds where our cries arose
            lost in the surging engines.

Yet the roomlight where we made our love
        still cubes us in amber. Out of the averaging
likeness, Pavlovian salivation at the bell
            of a nipple, our lives extract their

time-thread, our gospel-truth. While Holiday
        Inn and Exxon populate the stretch
between Washington and Richmond with lights,
            I rewrite our pasts in this present:

recalling your waking, dear wife, to find
        a nipple rosier, we not yet thinking *a child*
though impossibly guessing her features
            the feathery, minutely combed lashes

the tiny perfect nails, though not yet
        the many later trees at Christmas. Now
I know only backwardly, inscribing these sign-
            ings that fade as the ink dries.

Remembering the graphlike beading of darkness,
        I recall the ways that time once gave us—
distracted by signs for meals and clothing,
                travelers, heavy with ourselves

defining the gift that bodies carry,
        lighting the one, inner room, womb for
our daughter. Seeing from above, I read
             this love our child embodies.

Snapshot of Jonquils

My past labors lift their faces
        of blossom from a leaf-dross,
goldening the slope like laughter—
                like daughters rewarding me

within the language of these waters
        lower down, over stone, in a gloom
where years groan *going, already gone.*
              I stand not alone as the sun

holds the day's transience tenderly: its great
        sight not ready, quite, to crumple the snapshot
of these jonquils—as when the eyelid of horizon closes
            fast around the ball of night.

Escaping Gravity
for Houston Baker

My reclusive parents waited in thought
        to be waited upon by African American
servants. The farm passed along like a sacred
              obligation by my grandfather's father

(shot through the lung at Chancellorsville)
        was a burden to my father. Just before losing
his faculties, he bought other lands for tobacco.
            My daughter, fainting at his funeral,

embodied the southern lady. My mother-in-law,
        raised on a farm, won't throw anything away,
no matter how worn-out or useless. As I
           grow older, my accent thickens.

Accepting its sweetness and bitter illusions
        I've lived four-fifths of my life in this South
that believed in a lie we all still suffer for.
           This long-owned land owned men.

While selling the farm, I drove with my wife
        to Lexington, Virginia, and the shrine of Robert
E. Lee. His myth had proved too powerful,
           like a black hole's force field.

Assembling his family around him in death,
        it drew back a daughter, who'd married,
from her graveyard in North Carolina,
           to that home soil that southerners

feel in their bones as their final destination.
        We'll take our own stand here, against
those legions of gray reenacters charging up
           Cemetery Ridge. We'll dedicate

our final years to clearing those delusions
        that rise from unmarked graves, like the yellow-
fever miasma that Jamestown settlers
           tried to disperse with cannon.

Charles, James Winstead, let's all come home
           and reclaim our native land. We'll
fish in Contentnea Creek. Together, we'll
               try to discover how rivers can

run to the coast, free of hog farm effluent
           and the stain my great-great-grandfathers
bled into fields, dying in the old lie of race.
               Their blood and their tragedy seeded

these graves—your ancestors and mine—into
           this history of soil that will remember.
I work to pay the debt due their coerced
               sweat: an obligation to understand.

The Headlines Fade

Not only daylight lets me read. This evening
        I watch, as legibility drains from the air
though oaks in the west print hieroglyphic
                traces on the white of a window.

The body of darkness settles downward with
        its fur. Bats squeak and flick in sparks
of black. Arthritic limbs mark
            a pearl-lustrous enlightenment.

Stars needle the enigma in baffled points.
        Slumber beasts rise and ride, witches
in snatches of worsted, the dragon bulging
            his lair, Medusa's disasters.

When in the final fading I switch on a bulb,
        the subliminal hauntings stretch and slink
from print in its orderly march. Blindly.
            Everything imaginable possible.

A Fictive World

They constructed a world by their will: my hieratic
       grandparents, instructing clearly in those things
they held dear, so I'd not be dissuaded of the belief—
            that the pecan tree feathery in leaf

might not rock the earth beneath it during storm;
       the barn though safe against harm, the chicken yard
charmed in its fence beyond so that the hens would nest
            there still in lightning and wind.

They contended for my soul, portraying with their play-
       farm in town a wholeness they knew already gone,
or always only an ideal. My grandfather plowed the rows
          of his garden with muscle alone,

man and mule, behind the plowshare with two handles
       and one wheel. The corn curved duly where he'd been.
The hens we fed with corn sat their basket-nests
          while our hands plucked eggs out warm.

He weighed me with his eye as I palmed the chalky
       oval and positioned it carefully in the crystal lattice
within his basket. He'd place one apple for my eye, the sky
          isolating its red on porch rail:

color I'd read the word by—as my nose understood
       ham from a woodburning range that cooked his meals.
I saw that hens, turned into roasts, first had their
          necks wrung by old Aunt Eliza

to run crazily about the yard pinpointing blood,
       collapsing soon. It wasn't a fairy tale I was told. Folk
got old, died, and hogs killed at the farm (the real farm)
          had their guts scraped clean in this

decency of a walled yard—the cellophane casings squeezed
       full with red-white lean-fat meat. Gray sage leaves
my grandmother grew cut the scent. Her sparse
          spice beds, squared with bricks,

raised two roses wandering in a partial shade that
       the wingtip feathers of the pecan tree made.

Scuppernongs twined the spread-wide head-high
                    scaffolding of split cedar posts.

Few were let enter there: me, my brother, Babs our
                    cousin, ten if I was eleven; Babs's father Sam and
Virginia her mother, whose cozy house past
                    the chickens' wire prison embraced

a smaller pecan we'd climb. Beyond the white board
                    fence of grandfather's yard was his goldfish pond.
There hyacinths grew, stems like the strands of Babs's hair
                    that Virginia would pull out to plait.

A cherry tree reflected on the water. Its fruit like red
                    marbles or tiny Christmas ornaments marked
sparkles on the surface, for the goldfish to flash under.
                    The cherries made me sick if I'd eat

too many but I would again, though mostly I received
                    the lessons they lived for me. Brown-headed, frowning,
I'm concentrating seriously in the summer scene in
                    the snapshot with Babs by the water.

My grandparents disbelieved change, arranging their time
                    so I'd see them sitting occupied, she peeling peaches
into a pan, him reading his Bible in the parlor, white hair
                    wispy in moving air—the scriptures

fixed in a black-leathered book as he followed suit, white
                    shirt and black-blue trousers after the early morning's
work. They wished to train my soul in their world:
                    the decorous Thanksgiving dinners

with silver and two candlelabra, the celery, deviled eggs,
                    pickles and olives in narrower and wider dishes, iced
tea in the cut-glass goblets on stems, the turkey sliced on
                    the sideboard by old Aunt Eliza.

Grandfather said the blessing and started the plates going
                    around. It is only strange to me now, this stage:
a frail wooden house where one board trembled in the hall
                    as I stepped, to jingle a handle

of the dining room sideboard. The props, just chairs for all,
            left the two of them solemn at either end—my mother
and father and Teaky and me on one side of the table,
                        Virginia and Sam and Babs on the other.

The rest of it drifts away. Aunt Eliza handles the candles
            like a spirit, then cuts the cake, passing slices
across a distance that grows greater between the sideboard
                        and the table. The clapboard walls

turn transparent and we float heavenward, circling
            the shiny mahogany within his blessing.
The singing lifts us, "Sunrise Tomorrow" on the parlor piano
                        and grandfather's hoarse tenor

beseeching me to believe, though already the grave earth
            seems deepening around him. Time is precious
while he sings, with those he will soon enough
                        be gone from. Now my grandson

wonders at this patience I assume, that I am willing
            to teach whenever he will listen. That I guide him
with our steps beside the stream, as we pick for my wife
                        trout lilies like nodding arrested

match flames. Inside again we hand him the colored
            letters of the alphabet as he is singing them and
arrange the magnetic ABCs around the iron table
                        in our screened-in porch. He touches

them and says he understands. When he goes home
            his mother calls to say he's writing his letters!
But we have no tree like a feather duster, no fishpond,
                        no garden with corn, no fenced yard

for discreetly butchering hogs. We watch a few TV
            programs together. The world has turned many times
around since then, yet I'm with my grandfather again
                        when my wife and I sing with Christian.

I sympathize with my grandparents' lies. They'd wished
        to hide a rush beyond the fence, though their
bodies let down their own defenses, grandmother's first.
                    The past they led me to worship is lost.

But the tale of them teaching me lasts, their lies against
        time, the sublime sad tenor of their ways now
trembling in a space like a house made of cards.
                    The wind in their yard remains,

the pond, the hams hung up pungent and smoked in a dark
        beside the shed where grandfather propped his tools.
From them I relearn how a touch which imparts belief
                    makes its own truth. My mouth

with the tastes and speech their fictive practices fed here
        shapes its own words, accepting fraud, and loves
those who died denying change—fighting that last rear-
                    guard action we all are falling in.

Imagining Kitty Hawk

Here on the coast I imagine Kitty Hawk—
        and those first, sand-bumping flights when
Orville and Wilbur predicted control of that open
                horizon—my American brothers.

So now they'd succeeded, Huck and Tom Sawyer
        aloft, innocent in their genius, fearing women,
impatient of conversation with the stuffy nobles.
                Yet impressive, well read, not quite

the noble savages, gracious and diffident, lifelong
        bachelors turning miserly with invention:
riding the precarious currents, preaching by example
                to the top hats, monocles, and furs.

The doubled planes of linen, ash, and spruce
        afforded a rare pulpit for Wilbur—who'd assisted
Milton, his bishop-father, in suing the United Brethren
                in Christ. Balancing their machine

in midair, one brother from Dayton rocked all Europe:
        free of the Cain and Able competition, adroit
in gusts, cognizant of coefficients of drag and lift,
                self-reliant Emerson of experiment.

Free of the small theater of the antique, the sleepwalking
        of the Middle Ages (as old Walt put it) Wilbur
sat still in the middle of the air as the twentieth century
                rushed past: inheritor of reenactment.

Beneath him in his mastery, the landscape
        festered with wealth and ambition. In six quick
years, a map-world trenched with ancient schism
                would burst its stitches, spewing corpses.

Then imagination again became an agony
        as sons of the sons of Milton Wright cleft a first
transparency of idea. Linen wings with machine guns
                scribed skies in spirals of burning.

Conversation in Faculty Commons

Discussing the bleak Second Law,
        we break the symmetry of knife and fork,
gesturing with napkins. Linda revolves an apple
               round as Earth, before her first bite.

Larry cuts his orange-sun, filling space
        with scented light. "A planet is a system—
like a person"—Linda muses. "Orderly. Feeding
             on energy. Off-loading entropy."

Though our rolls lose their piled height,
        strewing unavailably in crumbs, Mike lifts
celestial mechanics in deterministic
             orbits, leaving the will free on Earth:

"Newton avoided conflicting with theology.
        He bounced his billiards unpredictably."
"He sure had balls," winks Jimmy—the bones of Howard's
             chicken our memento mori.

I describe Coleridge's cat-harpsichord,
        simile of soul in its mechanistic body.
"It perched at the keyboard. A punched paper roll
             caused a key to go down. A paw

followed quickly." "So kitty doesn't add to the Romantic
        Liszt," smiles Howard. "When the world's a machine,
matter plays the tune," I insist. "The psyche believes
             it's composing old moon and June."

"If he imagined language determined, how did
        he write *The Ancient Mariner,*" asks Larry.
"Remember the dice," I say. "Seriously, he disavowed
             the material world. Locke to Berkeley."

"A drastic solution," grunts Mike, "when reading
        Newton would've saved his roast beef and pudding."
"Could an image in the mind of God be as tasty
             as organic molecules?" Howard chews.

"It's only being played by a more ethereal
        instrument," I conclude. "So," says Howard,

"still, there's no free will." "Unless poetic thought
                    arose spontaneously, in response

to a divine breath from nature," I suggest, "in an Eolian Harp."
        "So God would be source of wicked thoughts and
dirty jokes and children out of wedlock," Jimmy
                    chuckles. "But isn't he—or she—anyway?"

asks Linda. "Heisenberg's world seems to run on
            its own but is not predetermined," Larry states.
"Einstein didn't like it," Mike mutters. "Imagining
                    how freedom and order coexist—

that's beyond the physicist," says Howard.
        "Ever the chemist," answers Larry. "You identify
the organic sequence. But how did the atoms link up? How
                    organize themselves into the mouse?"

"Complexity theory," I reply. "If molecules catalyze
            mirror-image molecules, eventually you arrive
at DNA." "The chaos-people are overeager; they see
                    computers everywhere," Larry sighs.

"But that deeply complex math of instability
        is out there," I say. "In the weather. In falling
water. In turbulence over a wing." "He's getting us
                    to airplanes," Jimmy winks. "To win

the air war again." "I just think that the butterfly-wing
        effect magnifies quantum uncertainty. It gives
the universe an openness," I say. "But to *what?*" Larry
                    asks. "There's God's plenty of mystery

in physics." "What he's after is a kind of joint, where
        meaning may enter creation," Howard puts in.
"Yes. Haven't you noticed how physics replays Genesis?" I ask.
                    "In the beginning was the Bang,"

Jimmy intones, plosively. "Eden was our time in the trees,"
        I continue. "God directed evolution to consciousness.
That was the Fall. Awareness of death." Linda gazes at
                    the apple she has bitten. "But what

small inputs direct evolution?" she asks. "It's all survival
            selection," Mike growls. "Must be something more,"
I sigh, rising. We make the ritual trip for a second
                        cup, then turn to old anecdotes and jokes.

"We learn new facts every day," Larry muses, relaxed
            in his chair, with coffee. "That we're made of star-ash.
That continents drift. The age of the universe. Galaxies
                        more billions of years ago, through Hubble."

"But when and why will the compounds of the mouse
            return into their elements?" Mike grouches. "Any system
preserving itself against the down-flux of entropy
                        temporarily swims against the stream."

They talk about retirement, these fatherly friends,
            not so much older, or wiser. Howard's eyes limit
his reading. Mike recommends a surgeon. He had his own
                        hernia repaired—after ten years.

I see that one strand of pasta snakes my broccoli-
            tree, my garden peas. Gripped by the forces we discuss,
we accept our contentment—thermodynamics in shambles
                        around us—leaving disorder to the waiter.

Charles

Charles remained my special friend, brown kid
        I'd played with beside the station when he was
ten and I eleven. A vacant lot between his house
                and our Esso pumps kept the dumped oil

in hollows. Weeds scattered up the hill of our castle
        where we huddled behind a parapet that crumbled
like brown sugar. The dirt rested thin and washed-over
            so fennels rose singly in feathers

that we could crawl between, not staining our knees.
        We strung oil cans on wires and pulled them for wheels,
then sat on the five-quart ones for stools or thrones. The last
           little oil we trickled into bottle caps

resembled molasses. We pretended to drink it—dark amber
        and syrupy but not a color to stain you. Charles's house
felt sparse when he fed us soda crackers spread with mustard.
           We understood not to be seen together

too much by my father or Charles's mother. We'd lie back
        and talk in the back seat of a Buick or a Cadillac waiting
shiny and empty for its owner. We'd stay low knowing not
           to track sand on the upholstery or carpet.

Charles and I kept in touch for years, seeing each other
        when I'd be working the station at night, lounging
before closing up on piled tires beside the hydraulic jack,
           near water cans and the lug wrench.

He'd sit on the bench with a beer in a paper sack
        from Rooster's Esso across the street and we'd talk,
almost like before. I didn't drink yet but had a girl.
           We thought pretty much the same

about things. He knew I didn't like to make the black
        guys take a paper cup to drink from the electric
cooler so we'd both lounge there sipping and talking
           without ever mentioning the issue.

I saw him only a few times after I started college.
        That last summer I worked the station, I knew he'd

been away and returned. He'd learned welding
                    in a shipyard in Norfolk and spoke

with not quite the same accent. When he paid for the packs
          of gum and condoms I noticed his right thumb
gone. Answering the look in my eyes he said
                    "That was before. That was the sawmill."

I remembered he'd handled lumber just across the road
          when I was a senior in high school. "It was my start.
My first hard work" he said. "Same as my Dad" I said.
                    "But he lost the ends of his fingers

in the belt of the compressor." "I reckon I'll go back
          up there and work for the government" he said,
his chocolate eyes shiny with intelligence.
                    "I'll miss Saturday nights down here."

His nub thumb squeezed my own thumb's knuckle
          like the secret handshake of a club. This initiation
feels firmer as the years pass—like that day in D.C.
                    seven years ago when I swear I saw

his eyes and head in the black man crossing a street,
          hunched, wearing the embers of hope in the burnt-
looking cloth that hooded his face like a monk's.
                    Charles, our trust is gone—that equal

look, man to man. That is what I mourn my friend
          as I reach for my wallet on M Street—for the sad alms
that never atone for our loss. These men have all their
                    thumbs. I never shake their hands.

The Wizard of Oz

Boiling up with smoke like the Wizard of Oz
        against his curtain he appeared in Pearl
Harbor air, his jaunty fedora and cigarette holder
                burning bush to our woundedness.

Father in a wheelchair, he bore the burden of *us,* voice
        arcing the wrecked antennas, booming for impotent guns.
Wholly his at last, democracy's arsenal, we'd phoenix
            new planes from the flaming wings.

Victory arose as he spoke, his aristocratic profile
        healing that skyline of jagged metal. He warmed
December with the Hawaiian lagoon of our dead,
            enunciated our course in the worst

the nadir. In Yamamoto's breast the Rising Sun set
        in strategies of desperate risk, defeat what he'd
studied at Harvard. The wonder was *our* hearts,
            the *remember* they quoted on production

lines and training fields as Jackie Cochran's WASPS
        ferried hot F-6Fs from the Grumman Iron Works
to San Diego. A face like a cloud-top overlooked
            the country in its divisions, Commies

wildcatting North American and its B-25s, Henry Ford
        a crusty seventy-seven, unwilling to make Merlins
for the hated Brits. FDR, pampered patrician forever in
            other women's company, assumed

this worry, wheeling invisibly within the clouds, his
        baritone electrifying the sixty million cat's-whisker
antennas he stroked for sparks. God-sex voice,
            he roused us to chamber the cartridge,

to kill in his name. He saw us each across the desk
        in his fireside chats, him the delegated coherence
his country lacked—though he also illusion. Missy
            LeHand, amanuensis, imagined

herself his wife. He was lifted toward sleep, nights,
        by a black man from Warm Springs, who straightened

his withered legs on the lone twin bed. Eleanor thought
                    he and Winston made war too much a game

yet when English Tars and American Swabs held the same
         hymn books on the *Prince of Wales,* Roosevelt and
Churchill underwent a mystical marriage. Two wills,
                unified, magnified the choruses.

He'd kept quiet about Einstein's letter. A father, he did
        what he had to do, what he could. He killed
and lied and refused the Jews. And we'd win with him as
             coach, our excuse, the silk ribbon

on his pince-nez the noose around the Axis' windpipes.
        So "Pa" wheeled his White House corridors in supreme
isolation, the unconditional surrender beyond—grail-ideal
           in air as he failed—the Bomb his

orphan. What was it but performance, theater in clouds,
        words broadcast through skies causing planes to arise—
talk the magical act shouted back and forth across the Atlantic
         and Channel by the hideous madman

and the Anglo-American prima donnas? A splintered Logos
        fumbling toward apocalypse mumbled *Hamburg, Dresden.*
Then in the mouth of honest uncertain Harry became a stutter.
         Hiroshima he blurted. Then halted.

An unwilling ghost beyond the Enola Gay, Franklin groaned,
        as a new sun lit the lone B-29's wing.
His guilt was mine, was all his sons'. The headline read
            like a giant sports outcome.

I roamed exultantly around the breakfast room as my
        mother put silently down the orange that reminded
her of a fireball. Our father stood gloomily with us,
           stiffly victorious, grave as iron.

Control Line Model

I studied piano after the war. My music teacher's
        brother visited from California, flying his scale
model Beech Staggerwing on the school's ball diamond
                one evening. An engineer, he circled

his perfect paradigm of a plane till its propeller
        and Olsen engine marked the edges of a vortex
with smoke: the turns its control lines swept like
                panes of water spiraling a drain.

Then the times sucked him back to San Diego, me taken
        fast in my father's car to classes at Duke University.
There I studied utilitarianism in ethics, the greatest
                good for the greatest number,

each particle of happiness a golden grain or globe
        or ant egg that each individual should scurry and
carry away though (impossibly) sharing—society a funnel
                we tumbled inside of, in jumbles.

Atoms knocked each other in deterministic patterns,
        a machinelike racket that was not music because
it rocked on aimlessly around an absent center—
                symphony without conductor.

Molecules piled like my books and records that summer
        in the first apartment, each piece of love and desire
slung by centrifugal force around a flyer no longer
                there, on his own home diamond.

Liebestod

"Blue Velvet" cupped us like heaven. Nat King
       Cole's cat's tongue, stroking our circles, felt
fiery with stars. Tony Bennett's "Because of You" parked
               our cars where fireflies winked.

A compass inside us vibrated toward their deep-veed
       Souths, poles of our worlds while we whirled,
to lyrics on spindles. Then broadcasts of news
           spun fabulous with H-bombs.

The father of a friend dug a shelter in his yard,
       used finally by the son for a grave seduction.
It saved no one because actors in musicals danced and sang,
           flaring up in celluloid fame—

like our ping pong balls, that if dented, we heated
       with a match. These Earths melted brightly to ash
if we held them too close—like us after MYF, kissing
           near the oak-sheltered church, whose

lore helped us sort out our fears, the lies and horrors
       from what might happen, tomorrow. The couple we'd
heard of had sighed-in carbon monoxide, her fingers still
           ringing his penis, stiff where it entered

her death. How could dives under desks save our lives
       from a hundred suns? As I worked underground
greasing cars, I thought of that ventilated tomb
           with its food and First Aid. The girl

who got laid down there had her fetus sucked out
       in some northern city. After labor in
the pit of desire, my radio solaced me
           with lyrics from afar—wired

the wide, star-abraded sky to a spindle inside.
       Through the frying static, Tony and Frank, Nat
and the Duke, wheeled our time away, in tune with their song—
           their Liebestod our lullaby.

The Comparison

Seeing ourselves as opposites, we felt always
        a comparison. We were sad and fragile said
mother, by the way she acted. They were hearty and glad.
                They bore easily what a white woman

just couldn't stand: the heat during those long hours
        before the stove, when the back of one hand
pushed back the sweaty tresses (our Teenie hid
                sweat and her hair with a kerchief);

and the anxieties of family. Teenie said her daughter
        in the penitentiary had a "scholarship." "She peel
apples," Mother repeated, not as a cruelty,
                she thought, but to show how blacks

didn't worry—their happy-go-lucky demeanor
        a true reflection of how different they were.
We pretended not to believe in their depth of emotions—
                their moans and loud crying at funerals

a show, we said, like the minstrel joking when we'd
        feel solemn and blue. We thought only of ourselves:
living inwardly, suffering perplexities, inexplicable griefs
                while they lived simply, outwardly.

We, the high, wore whites and grays and browns, they
        the low purple, fuchsia, scarlet, and chartreuse.
We walked tight, they moved loose—they like night, we the day—
                circled like light on their river.

We brooded over ownership and money, extracting
        a cash crop each season from the used land
through tobacco plants, the roots invading like an alien
                species, the ranks of leaves a garish,

tropical verdigris. They seemed happy with the day's
        green bills when work along the steaming rows,
between stalks like soldiers at attention, had ended.
                They'd buy beer with one dollar, food

with the other, and a little bit left for the "chillun"—
        not worrying about tomorrow we thought, worrying

about our own uncertain future. All depended on them
                    who might show up at six A.M.

to ride out of town in the back of a pickup, or might not.
          We seldom saw them melancholy, unless hungover,
working through the extra sweat standing on their faces
                    like rain beading the hood of a truck—

the pain-grimace showing as a rueful half-smile
          as if even then, with every muscle aching, they might
break out laughing or into a joke or a song. Tense and lonely,
                    nursing superior grievances, we hid

our losses and rejoicings with deliberate faces.
          They displayed everything, every moment's splendor
when cropping a row was finished and a cloud came
                    over, the side of a nearby thunderhead

like an ice cliff rising into distance, where swallows
          arced in specks—them smiling with abandon then
drinking water from a Mason jar, some of it spilling from
                    corners of the mouth, darkening the shirt

where it wasn't already soaked. They'd whoop at each other
          across two fields, while we kept our voices low
unless issuing orders. They seemed unruly, careless, not
                    to be depended on, while we were

shopkeepers of virtue, adding up our good deeds like money.
          We scorned how they'd forget to check the oil
in a tractor, how they'd drive their own cars without
                    a good battery, sharing jumper cables

communally. We misunderstood their vitality,
          seeing their joy as quixotic, endlessly elastic.
We scorned and envied their sexuality
                    that they laughed about, seriously.

Their race was always with us, we thought,
          our good and bad luck, an inheritance, part
of the landscape of leisure that our white columns
                    founded on their backs and knees.

We heard their voices as choruses, hymns ancient
            as the Earth, or as the jive tune of our dreams.
Only once did we see we couldn't see, or hear.
                        A rumored body haunted all

conversations, a Negro shot (of course) by the sheriff—
            he a horse of a man, mechanic for my father
in daylight, who worked his girth down alleyways,
                        near the neon cafe, at night.

At the inquest he asked us to share in his
            illusion, to see the close limb-twining of that juke
joint Saturday night as the cause for a killing.
                        What Wiley'd said he'd seen

was never found: the razor quickly flicked
            from a pocket. The dead youth held a comb
in his hand. Though cleared of blame by a judge,
                        Wiley resigned in shame and

our community closed around the news like a lake
            around a drop of rain. Nothing remained, no relic
of the deceased, no nickname, no recollection of his
                        figure or gesture or expression.

No whisper, only a blank like the often-charred
            pine headboards of a cemetery out in the country.
I drove there to think, to stare at the faces of wood
                        that seasonal fires had erased

of vines and lichen. Among my ancestors' names
            I saw a vacancy past color, heard a soundlessness
past voice: the fact of a life lost, of a youth now
                        hardly more invisible to us.

I thought of those earlier family servants,
            surrogate daughters and sons, unhonored nurses
buried without notice, denied by blindness, one
                        color not seeing past the mask

of the other. Among the stones of this deafness
            I felt thorns on my ankles like iron.
Far in the silence, a mourning dove remembered
                        the tone of their song. A mortal grief.

Southern Humor

Jokes about the South come easy, these lazy
        days. What could be funnier than a half-million
wounded and killed, or dead of typhoid or starved
            in defense of keeping slaves?

The Ku Klux Klan just tickles some funny bones
        and it's always a horse laugh to hear how
rural children lag in school. The gasoline splash
            on churches up pine-lined lanes

still boils against skies in billows of humor.
        The joke's on us if a four-year-old drifted
hours in a boat, because his father went under,
            vainly trying to rescue his cousin.

Sin seems especially southern, like the idiot's peek
        or look of paranoiac aunt past her parlor curtains.
Usually no one's there. This place is a myth so the horrors
            we expect condition what happens—

like the driver's foot slipping off the brake,
        the van with its six more children going down
the bank toward Susan Smith's two sons. We're
            laughably worshipful of maternal piety

especially when it's proved so murderous. Shrines
        to our losers fill courthouse squares and shelves
of menagerie glass, from William's Mississippi
            to Williams, Tennessee.

Nothing tickles the ribs so much as laughing till
        you cry, telling one more whopper about Dolly's
double burden. Those mountains of milk and honey
            that never would run dry

now trickle down vinegary waters, as we suck on
        apples of fallen orchards. We dream the moon-
whitened nipples, on bolsters that snow their feathers
            along labyrinths of family trees,

where white-suited Kentucky colonels lead fried chicken
        battles and a few little Lees sell lots of cars,

all used. It's a land so full of stand-up comics
                              we're competing with the Jews.

What we have left to lose is only new money
          that bought the old honor. We're like a baby so homely,
we hang these jokes around our necks like pork chops
                              so the country hounds will lick us.

At Greenfield Village

Like a ball bearing bouncing in its groove, I drive
          the broken pavement to Greenfield Village—ideal
not present in history. Opposite *Technical Review*
                    I park near serpentine brick, look

over an opposite wall, into an antique world.
          The locomotive hoots its smoke, a windmill
whirls its vanes among apple trees of Henry Ford's
                    first home: a past as it was,

as it might have been. A baked-bread innocence haunts
          the faces of children and parents I enter among.
I pay to see the family happiness America had promised.
                    Walking the graveled streets as if a boy,

I approach the Firestone farm, watch a dragonfly
          not on anyone's payroll. It hovers calves while
they're looked at by children. I sit under a black
                    locust tree, see swallows circle

a cornfield. A past is here represented. The effort
          of cooking, of water for bathing, of lamplight for
evening, the plowing, fencing, sewing, exhausts
                    the women as well as the men. All wears

a nimbus of meaning. Held by this dream-perimeter,
          I return to my own home village. The steam engine
passes like a sequence of memories. The sawmill, the pottery,
                    these houses with looms, preserve

old patterns. I pass unripe Concord grapes, apple trees
          with green hard scarred fruits. Enter the birthplace.
The hall, with odors of soap and woodsmoke, holds
                    a woman in period costume.

Orville and Wilbur's bicycle shop and house
          appear out back, where no automobile disturbs
the bemusement of these streets. Sun-dapple from maples
                    thickens within densities of history.

Here, as Emerson predicted, the mechanical and
          pastoral coexist, at peace. In Edison's lab

filaments glow, a fictional sequence of development
                    preserving the specimen days in vials.

The village has its small South: two slave cabins
          from Georgia, a depression-era tenant shack,
the Home of Stephen Foster and, on the pond,
                    the Suwanee Steamboat escorted by ducks.

In America, anything seemed possible, even
          the salvage and restoration of time. A homestead
that Henry found no future in stands fragile with
                    nostalgia, like the Wrights' linen wings.

Outside, the velocity of the multitude of cars
          cleaves parks from the neighborhoods. The eyes
of drivers at a caution flash on and off, alert
                    and blank, in the binary flicker.

The face of an absent father disperses in ozone,
          eyesockets bruise-blue, cheeks mere puffs
above the concrete cloverleaf, the mouth a jet-line:
                    white, wind-cut, smiling at nothing.

The F-117 Nighthawk at Wright-Patterson
for Khaled Mattawa

Piotr Ufimtsev's flat-bottomed diamond
       evades detection, a thought-apparition
born like Athena. Its matte skin drinks
           light like the dark in my telescope.

So secret that its pilots lied to their wives
       unfaithfully, it erases itself from radars:
manta of theory, negating space, changing
           air war from *genocide* to *strategy*—

the tragedy of the civilian shelter only
       faulty intelligence. The fear in its cockpit
for the six-hour mission, sucked into instruments,
           calibrates landscape to absence.

Polishing lenses to an obliterating clarity
       it hovers in judgment, revealing itself like
Jupiter to Semele: tangential to experience
           except for those on earth when they explode.

The Cape

Floridly handsome, neo-Wagnerian, major
        in the SS, you finished the war in a body
cast—surrendering yourself and your men and
            rocket plans to the U.S.

Faustian von Braun, the Party hardly mattered,
        or country—Earth for you a launching site.
Though you turned Christian in Huntsville, space
            flight remained your religion—

Canaveral another Peenemünde. In our race
        to the moon, we forgot the dooms you'd arced
on London. Bombed, you built V-2s with slave
            workers tunneled into a mountain.

I had praised with my father the force and height
        of your Saturn rocket. Later I visited the Cape
and walked along the beach, mindful of the Icarus-feathers
            of flamed metal. Waves healed

seamlessly while I felt the perpetual youth of hopes,
        the springs that Spanish explorers found in that air
where a vast blue overarched the Vertical Assembly
            Building, giant shed of Saturn.

A caterpillar-crawler hauled rockets like mountains
        to be thrown against heaven. Recalling my father's
words I admired the launching pads, concrete squares
            in dunes beside the solicitous towers—

their distancing thinness sketching in metal
        a skeletal aspiration. So I had wished against
horizons, driving in a fierce trip west
            while von Braun's plans unfolded

toward the moon. So I had stared beyond canyon
        rim, across sixty-mile vistas toward mesas,
partisan still of my father's will for the future.
            So I had cheered on Wernher's

people, this family of Americans and ex-Nazis
        that raised our flag above the airless craters.

I watched Neil Armstrong's one small step for
                    man from a bus station in Denver.

So as I printed my feet along the Cape I
          thought of my father and von Braun, two men akin
in hope. I watched the Shuttle distantly on its pad,
                  fuel tank a cocoon against

its belly, spun a moth-brown. After a huge
         shuddering, porcelain wings would emerge,
flying the inferno-blossom. I told my father of
               the launch, watching his eyes light up.

Mourning his failing, I purchased a prescription,
         while the command module finished its falling,
and trails of the separating rockets diverged
             like the horns of Michelangelo's

Moses—ours the hubris of artillery-shell-shaped
         Mercury shot over the horizon, of Apollo
and Saturn—gods heel-winged with combustion,
             stuttering their oxygen-reactions,

thrusting Christa McAuliffe into myth.
         Wernher was one of us, denying tragedy
with a hope so powerfully ignorant, Earth stares
             his blue iris blindly into space.

Space at the Table
for Christian

This year of the divorce, we adjust to new
        space at the table. Winter intends an end
as I ponder my grandson's future, poignant
               as his one forgotten glove.

December wanes in windows eastward
        where fall's hurricane cleared sky-room.
Ceylon and Keemun console a cold ache while
            we string these boughs with lights.

Outside, galaxies snow and spin like flakes
        in a wide storm. Faces reflect in ornaments
fragile as the sphere of air. Smiles stretch along
            each green and red equator.

Gathered for Christmas, we kiss across distances
        as inscrutable frankincense and myrrh place
our senses in spirals, recessions. Coordinates
            of spruce and orange-scent

intersect as Nativity. We hear tidings that
        the world's strange stage means to hold this
treasure—each seeing each in brief meeting across
            our table in the expanse of night.

Grandfather Wordsworth

You remembered waiting for the horses that would
        bear you to the death of your father—the day
tempestuous dark and wild, your companions
                a single sheep, a blasted hawthorn.

Reinventing this proleptic sorrow, you knew
        the hanged murderer, a woman with pitcher
on her head, garments vexed and tossed
                by a wind of visionary dreariness.

This intensity sanctified loss, lifting violet by
        a stone into poetry. On Grasmere peaks
you climbed near stars, fathered yourself from
                the living nothingness past hearth fires

and language. You hated Robespierre,
        learned guilt, knocked sense into the gilded diction
of your day with "Sir Patric Spens" and Coleridge's Mariner.
                Your voice spoke familiarly to me

from a school anthology. The scenes your words
        had painted moved, I knew from inside it another
climate and time. You inspired my first few poems—
                you and the good doctor Williams.

Next year, walking to Grasmere felt lonely
        and free, sunshine thin in late summer. Stephen
Gill at the museum outlined your favorite walk,
                William, with Dorothy: away from

Dove Cottage, around the lake, over a small mountain,
        and back. When I looked down from that peak
on Grasmere Lake, I felt complete. Words in my inner
                hearing spoke. Ancestors moved,

their moods raged and ranged in rain and
        blown mist. Grandfather Wordsworth, your wind
hit with sleet mixed in, rattling my poncho
                with a blast out of Scotland.

Wandering wherever it blew me I faced into ice,
        seeking the highest place, a farther pasture—

clambering walls, forcing my steps through
                    gorse that pierced my socks

toward the tarn with sheep like wooly boulders.
          Clouds gone, rainbow over, I covered a scrawny
hemlock with my sky-colored poncho and walked apart—
                    the wind then drying it, flickering it

into blue flame. The name then streaming my breath,
          William, held your name and my wife's
against the Atlantic distance. This banner
                    of desire carried me to Liberty's

for a William Morris fabric, then to Windsor where I
          purchased the antique scuttle, once too dear as
we'd admired it, together. Casting love into these,
                    I winged with the quick days home.

The scuttle shines today on our hearth, worth more or less
          as we remember or forget. Men were *immortal
and omnipotent*, Shelley whispers, if *Intellectual Beauty*
                    haunted us in permanence.

Did he ask if my gifts could recompense
          my wife for loving her intensely in absence?
We met at the airport, William, our embrace
                    like Eve's and Adam's, after.

Bells for Cecilia

The dead shall live, the living die,
And Music shall untune the sky
—A Song for St. Cecilia's Day

We visit Cecilia's effigy: the body
        Maderno observed on the opening of her coffin.
The three strokes cleft her neck, left
                the flowerlike head sagging

on its stem. A robe enfolds her, hips high in
        the side's bow. She gazes through a gauze
of pleated marble. Later we walk the Botanical
                Gardens where sun like a sword

touches necks of roses. Their seventeenth-century
        pedigrees struggle in drought. We breathe
a diesel stain this Roman afternoon
                wandering in airs of catacombs.

I picture those Eves and Adams of the Villa
        Borghese—and regret all cherished wounds,
sainthoods for those who'd rouged such tombs, flayed
                in tragedies Christ must redeem.

But where did the line begin? A pagan vein
        erupting in the Villa unearths the rape
by Hades as he grips Persephone. Hand in hand,
                long married, we follow the sunlight

as its quick blade slices each neck. At home
        under smoky azure, we descend the piazza
and sit by a wall, ordering *acqua* and a Coke—
                in love with the surface our day sends.

Stone of that time cools our skin. Ochre
        over stucco modulates with bells for Cecilia.
We think Bernini-marble: thigh of our
                season indented by Hades' fingers.

War Surplus Machine: A Dream

The night before selling my father's farm I have
        this dream. Holding a wrench he has crawled
beneath an olive-drab war-surplus truck used for
            hauling tobacco to market.

When his head and shoulders are hidden by fenders
        and hood I step up on the running board and
the blocks slip, the weight coming down on him
           in his heavy breathing. I reset

another jack under the axle but try as I may
        can't prevent the load's slowly crushing him
though he never cries out. Hearing his breathing grow
           labored and thick, I try to make

excuse, saying that again he's lost in his war-work
        as it conceals his stoic jaw and neck while the burden
increases. But I had so much wished to lift this
           obligation imposed by an era—

this awkward leftover the color of propaganda
        those decades ago. I think when I'm dreaming
that the whole thing's my fault—because I'm unable to break
           the contract I made to sell the farm.

So I surrender to events, drive home as if going
        to his funeral again, and sign the deed—leaving
our holdings by right of bone, in a field-cemetery that has
           buried our name since 1810.

The Deed

On the deed dated 1890, script of my great-
        grandfather assigns these lands to his son William
Henry *for his preferment in marriage.* The hand
              of my father has written across:

Old Home Place. As I unfold the rusty paper,
        the map tears partly in half. Too often
creased, this past is tenuous in my hands.
              Beginning at Toisnot Swamp then

southwest for eighty-six chains, this farm defined
        for a time to come would cross the highway
during my grandfather's boyhood. There past the homeplace,
              it included a stretch of railroad

and bent at the pine I remember: tree-Titan felled
        by the right-of-way crew. The original claim,
              through scrub oak and blackberry tangle, followed
              a swamp-line's dividing streams,

to anchor on a pine no longer standing.
        It read one hundred and eighty-six acres.
Concluding the contentious sale, I was forced to see
              twenty of the acres I had believed in

vanish. What was the truth of this place? My lawyer
        cousin explained. In the days of inexact *poles*
and *chains*, the makers of deeds envisioned
              more land than existed. Schooled in a family

that lined itself as from a dawn time, I accepted
        an earlier division: that fracturing of holdings
distributed among sisters—our lands bounded in
              by the married-to Bagleys, Crockers,

and Thompsons. Though the legacy of my grandfather's
        and father's farm had dwindled from its origin,
like lightwood concentrating in a rotting stump,
              I believed that a core stood secure.

How old was I when I first tried to embrace
        this pine like the world ash in Gilgamesh?

It lay rotting all my teenaged years, during the ritual
                    inspection of the boundaries of hope

with my father. These lands he wouldn't
          yet tend, while his own father lived,
held his story of the future. Though
                    his income lessened, the farm

promised riches—though run-down, eroded, the homeplace
          lived in by tenants, in need of repairs. It became our
inheritance, source of his maintenance when disabled—
                    then legacy for my ailing brother.

So I have been forced to face this myth, to accept
          whatever value the current world assigns to
this space of earth, with its poisonous history.
                    The will of one John Applewhite

transmits to his children, John, Martha, Elisha,
          and Isaac, along with the household furnishings,
certain human beings. Beedy, Lewis, Offy;
                    Wealthy, Feruba, Bright; Tabitha

Mereca, Jinna, and Litha—I write your names again
          here, since the many burnings of the iron-fenced family
graveyard have erased whatever chalked letters
                    once named you on the blackened

boards of heart pine. But your story will last, among
          the flaking fallible marbles, the names carved there
of Jonathans and William Henrys, the iron Confederate
                    States of America marker at one

grave's foot. Their rectangle of myth was sold prior
          to my own small betrayal, dispersed with the displaced
Scots, Irish, English, as they forgot old lore,
                    erased each season by plowing,

their enduring inscription only *cotton, corn, tobacco,*
          the shorter lines of gardens singing *beans, okra,*
collards, and *squashes*. Owning others, they forgot
                    good works, the fierce predestination—

becoming Old Testament Christians, attaching
        themselves to these fields like a new seed　.
of Abraham—beginning again with a war
                of division. When defeat had decided

their fates, they clung to these thorn-grown
        acres with a tenacity beyond hope. I refold
the map with its tear, remembering the shifting, uncertain
                lines my father showed me: road

pushed over by use, by a ditch the new practices
        grassed, the swamp-stream switching its channels
like a snake when you chop its head off, twisting in dirt.
                So I've sold a part of my heart

to compound in stock funds for my brother's keeping—
        this farm I ran for six years, in my father's
name, to fund his last seasons. The nursing home
                spread like his memory of fields:

one room a tree-cornered nook for soya beans or corn
        where the bobwhite fed—for cuneiform deer-prints
in soft soil at sundown. He saw it all in the halls around that
                wheeled throne he called his Cadillac.

He recognized faces of old friends in orderlies, saw
        Mother as the lady in a wheelchair who vanished.
Those fields of his head are gone with his vision. Those
                that spread in July heat and freezing

December, under loblolly pine, down clay-poor declivities
        toward Toisnot water, will continue to be owned by
raccoons, foxes, bobwhites, and deer—the only
                labels of possession I'll need

for that spot of earth henceforth. Already
        back fields too wet for plowing are
feathering themselves with broomsedge, preparing
                for the new generations of pines.

Rehearsal in Wallace Wade Stadium

No high heels and
stockings in these February stands.
No silk scarves. But trombones
glitter as Bud Wilkinson's son,
near a Gothic clock tower's stone,
returns in the sunlight of a run.
Or earlier, with my father,
I hear the single-wing formation gather
its choral glory as Billy Cox
fades back to the cheerings' *vox
humana*. Like Zeno's arrow,
the football spirals toward a receiver
and instants between presents narrow,
without the pass ever
vanishing into his hands.
As cymbals clash to the brim,
October in the stadium
subsides while the band finds its theme:
one flute-note shining through time.
The boy—an old grad's son—
remembers he is professor at the tone.

Reading the Stars

Nights near chill Orion, I haul out
        the long-barreled telescope, its three-
legged mount my companion. I climb up
             outdoor stairs, to a clearer view.

Jupiter's moons arc out differently,
        mathematical points, four bright
stones on invisible rings—engaging my
            thoughts with blindness and seeing.

But now the Trapezium: dust cloud in Orion's
        sword, where I stare into tiniest finitudes—
birth-glints in the uncanny placenta.
            They tremble in the eyepiece

as Earth's rotation moves the cannon-
        like barrel. Stars I know slide past,
succeeded by stars like dust of diamonds.
            I shiver in the damp air,

whispering of the double helix as story
        of origin. Strands separate, each catalyzing
its complement, the genetic message copied
            onto RNA. Adenine, thymine,

cytosine, guanine. I look backward for an end.
        Timespace answers with echoes. Self-similarity
in lightning, trees, arteries, rivers
            branches like revelation.

New stars swarm and hive in Orion,
        golden and platinum bees that fly to me
in photons—their honey this sense of *sense*—
            this syntax becoming sight—

this knowledge of being. And ending. They drive
        my body inside, to tremble within curtains,
while windows stare blankly at masses, where
            galaxies originate like hurricanes

in centripetal spirals. I rest with my wife
        among books and china, inherited furniture,

silver-framed photos of children, wooden beams from
                    a lost tobacco barn on the farm.

Established here, on this earth-crust adjoining
          a river, I watch, as behind our home
a ridge moves its rocky, tree-written edge
                    on the translucent almost-black.

The sortilege of branches casts our meanings
          from historical crookedness: fruits of light,
as from a Christmas tree in the window,
                    ornamenting space with belief.

The unendurable stars would show me my life
          and family through the wrong end of the telescope.
We seem to move across the dark, inscribed on
                    Orion in the observing instant.

Then time-orders separate. I see us projected,
          in our human perspective, back into the first
timescape. Our blood branches from the eyes of stars,
                    gazing back on original mysteries.

White Lake Last Light

Awake from the dream, I see us leave
        the grove, sixteen and eighteen, surrendering
ourselves to the pier-side crowd. I want
                the two we were, voyeur who

enters with lapsed light, yellow, surprised
        at us, together. Earlier we'd floated
belly to belly in an innertube, the lake
             pulled around us like a condom.

Thighs come at us veed like boat wakes,
        every girl's bulge across her pelvis holding
a future by Jack or Buddy. I shoulder
             us onto the turning wheel:

lights like a galaxy pivoted in scaffoldings.
        We ride with it holding hands, going
back up into the past, our breaths in unison,
              falling forward into the future.

Again we lie by the capsized boat near water
        again we know in a tight slick rush
with the bulbs in motion against Earth's rotation
            how we two transcend ourselves.

Wheeling and sighing with the time between us
        we haunt our union, wishing vision
reentering the world-whirling sensation
            when we had enacted begetting

with the many rising dizzily up out of dark
        onto the youth arc on top, then descending
to memory, the shadowy water. Our eyes not
            despising the crowd go blind

with the giant striding. Small outside alone,
        knowing the others that time had crowded
to pilings, we join in that lap of night
            borne inside their August riding.

The Southerner in Space after Death

He rejoins an experience voyaging outward:
           southerner in space after death. Reliving
a larger story he recedes among galaxies
                  from his planet of garden and battle.

Beyond loneliness in the black vacuum, he reviews
           his creation in vistas of star-ash and ocean,
sees treks across savannas wearing changing faces
                  brain-cases bulging with languages.

He retraces his path from Africa to the Middle East
           then to rivers of the Dordogne, where he drew
in a cave at Lascaux, later to Angleterre with
                  the Conquest, and finally to this New

World where he joined his brother from the old hot
           Eden—still wearing the inherited sunburn—
though he had gone pale in the cold. Here one brother
                  owned the other, though from the distance

of Orion he accepts this tragedy among cataclysms
           of other stars and planets. Returning along a beam
that set out when Cretaceous behemoths gorged on first
                  angiosperms, he comes to a field

in Northern Virginia and hears voices arise from near
           Spotsylvania Court House. Bullets whiz like bees
above the Bloody Angle, sawing down a tree.
                He finds it strangely peaceful

this replaying of passion to the death, this loss
           of self into the larger belief, blindly, mistakenly,
among faces suffused with a fanatical crimson
                wrong with his region, at home.

Then beyond his trenches this southern spirit looks at
           the monument to men from Ohio, loving them,
regretting their deaths, though all deaths are necessary,
                the soon or late not so much different

amid the shifted spectra of galaxies in recession.
           Turning outward toward the universe from his former

location, he is conscious of his creation and of Creation
                                    from whence his destiny arose.

Feeling his reunion with the burst stars that synthesized
                his elements he follows the direction of dust as it
gathers into a sphere: forest and soil that his ancestors
                                    tilled, enriching fields with their story.

As the atoms that bonded his memory to this place
                disperse, the ghost tastes scuppernong grapes, sees
leaves of a vine beside his grandfather's garden. Chickens
                                    squawk as the old man feeds them.

Documentary

I picture the town photographically,
        carry its years in my head: glare–flood,
transparent gold that burned the wood
           of houses and churches fiercely.

A pane of noon fell full
        beyond the eaves like a substance, a crystal
metal encrusting leaves. Imponderable
          beginning made visible.

Together on the porch, our torso-shadows
        flattened on the planks like paint.
Deeper in, grandfather's silhouette
          printed the windows.

We suffered a Sunday light, so ideal
        we could not act within it, only exist
as a tribute to its history, only feel
          a judgment-glare persist

through seasons of mules and tobacco leaves,
        Thanksgiving parlors, black men harvesting
in chiaroscuro—perspective that deceives,
          unfathomed by remembering.

It is afternoon always, always the sun
        illuminates changeless ways. We've begun
the same day again, we strain to stay
          as once we were, we and they,

a photo in white and black, a pageant
        enacted through us, innate, inherited,
sun by sun, each moment. So caught,
          we're cave shadows projected

from paradigms behind: progenitors
        whose blazing substance empties the form
bequeathed. Farmers without futures, war-losers.
          Proprietors of time.

The Book of Evening
for Jan

Light lay on the page of the bed turned
            to evening. Silvered by a black-green,
panes cast us onto the yard. Night hovered
                        where a poplar towered, then began

descending in a slow draining, lawn,
            azaleas, and trees leaking minute by minute
into space. A swallow crossed the skylight;
                        beech leaves lost their outline.

Air looked on my words from afar,
            compassionate, graying, with the earth's turning.
Our room let the outside in with glass a star
                        could pierce. Slowly my reading

was taken from the book as I sat. Our sheet
            turned down marked one more day. A white
lay without print, for our bodies to write
                        their dreaming on all night.

Still an immanence thought our ending not
            complete, this dimming that might be morning
from its color on the lawn but was *becoming*
                        as we felt it, a hinge, of changing light.

Yates Mill Wheel

for Yates Mill Associates, Inc.

Stars on the pond like corn kernels split
        under the stones' great gnashing still float
from steadier centuries, when nights'
           surfaces bore their weights—

days of water-rush from the dam made powerful
        by a print like broken grains: elemental
bright bits that Creation had scattered,
          here reflected and regathered.

Likewise, Yates Millpond held local folk
        from wagons and buggies. Men would smoke
a corncob pipe while children splashed and laughed,
          with voices the millrace hushed.

So cracking and gathering the kernel-years, this mill
        founded a people by waters, where a wheel
and its whirling stones marked the times' returns,
          celebrating families' reunions.

Three stories trembled with the heavy grindstone.
        Wheat from the smutter higher ascended again
and cooled in the hopper boy. The bolter
          sifted it through a silk cylinder

till it floated the chute, fine enough for wedding
        cake. Men bagged flour, hearty, grinning,
then wagoned home this marrow of life,
          bread-bond between husband and wife.

The gift of this simple mystery is a trust:
        this energy of gravity that our ancestors thrust
over a wheel, from its storage in water,
          to grind the grains and saw their timber.

The force that pulled hydrogen into bright
        points of stars propelled water as a weight
onto the bucketed rim: the wheel as it whirled
          on its axis like the turning world.

So Yates Mill lives, an idea of order
           we learn better as we grow older, and newer
solutions complicate our hours—paging
                us just as we seemed to be hearing

the season's turning. Here at Yates Mill,
           a forest circle encloses the water still.
Heirs of the past, we'll continue a cycle
               by restoring this symbol wheel.

Rescued from neglect and a hurricane,
           the granite teeth will taste corn again.
Generations gathered on the millpond's shores
               will recognize those starry years.

Upstream from the Little River Reservoir
for the Eno River Association

Glancing from a turkey vulture's wheel and gliding,
past the cross-shaped print of a hawk on pavement,
I wave away the wires, the cell phone towers.
A Persian cat on the fence where state maintenance ends
looks cowled and eared like an owl.
The trail I follow is spidered and rocky,
flooded by a dove's call, a woodpecker's knocking.
Rain puddles plate it with light of another century.
The shadow who walks before me wears the hat-silhouette
of a farmer. Wind seethes the pine grove from long ago,
suggesting a way beside. Through the clearing, I first see
the ruin of their living: the cedars, the blackberry tangle,
the weed-wrapped timbers—the shade tree for workers,
so old, these recently seeded pines around seem
temporary as yesterday's newspapers. The forested
gully widens into a sunken road.
The crows' raucous ironies confirm its depth,
its difference of perspective. Struggling for breath,
I clamber from this great trench, that leads
past the Civil War. I switch path left,
toward a distant chainsaw's snore and rumble.

But I don't wake yet; the slant down
toward the river hushes the modern sounds.
February sun glitters colder on needles of saplings—
yellow-green, the color they've always been.
Then the horizon drives wedges of blue in between trees
all the way to the ground. Land falls away
to the North Fork, green water slow here as I come nearer.
A light plane flying above me wakes the grove-whispers.
Fluorescent surveyor's tape flutters like banners,
wind mixes the still-sounding crow-knowings,
the exhalations of branches in motion. Then
the blunt *slap slap* of a helicopter's rotors.
I absorb deep vistas of trees, alongside the river.

Going back, I follow a side path upward,
see antifreeze-colored water in a patio
swimming pool, hear a basketball dribbled on concrete.
I look, sigh, go back down the hill, a man
who is trailed by his shadow, receding into shadows.

The Little River shimmers with times in contrast.
This history I breathe is alive, exists to save.
When we reverence what we shall become,
we walk within the reservoir of time,
inhaling *origin* like oxygen.

A Chorus for Children's Voices

for Nathaniel Stookey and the North Carolina Symphony

Like soaring birds
      we rise above the clouds,
discovering greater sight
        in newborn light.

Suddenly in surprise
      we imagine wide as skies.
Though earth lies dense with cares
        our horizon nears the stars,

where a brightness circling round
      rings in perfect endless sound.
Here crystal sun rays chime
        the whole of time.

ML